The Last Moments of the Night

Abbie Thacker

BookLeaf Publishing

Presentation by *BookLeaf Publishing*

Web: www.bookleafpub.com

E-mail: info@bookleafpub.com

ISBN: 9789357445238

First edition 2022

Before the Night Time

It's rather difficult to describe grey, the colour of clouds on a miserable day, tinged with pink just above the horizon. Grey is dull, murky and pale, a reminder of dreary rain on a stormy afternoon, almost white against the dark green leaves of windswept trees. In stories, the skies are always bright and blue and clear, only changing for pathetic fallacy, before returning to sweet summer's embrace. But there is something remarkable in an ordinary, grey sky. It may be nothing compared to the senseless darkness of night or the changing hues at sunset, but there is beauty, nonetheless. It conceals the true nature of the heavens, smothering the stars with light, hiding the gods behind a layer of cold. The breeze bends to its command, swaying between the feathers of pigeons, magpies, blackbirds. It flitters, unseen by mortal souls, swerving around the hardy brick houses, blowing gracefully over the smoothest of oceans. In lands unconquered by parasites, it remains untamed, fierce, desperate to reclaim the ashes of the earth, to rekindle a spark of passionate intensity. Grey makes the world more real, easier to digest, enchanting when compared to the ordinary sky. The tinge of pink, a sour taste against the grey and green, the colour of washed-out blood, a testament to the sunset which will soon rise, the golden hues ageing the landscape. It lifts the dull sky, a promise for a time where grey will be forgotten. Perhaps there will be red and yellow and orange, maybe colour will leap across the horizon, painting it with wild shades of natural patterns, a splattering of a melting rainbow. But for now, in the mundane harshness of daytime, there is grey.

At sunset, the sky turns to candlelight, a soft, orange glow dusting the very edges of each cloud like a shadow made entirely from angelic light. Already, the sky is clearing, making way for the moon and the stars, pale blue ever-darkening, reshaping, reborn into catastrophic night. Blue, the colour of a dying ocean, of forget-me-nots hiding from a thunderstorm, of the sky in every corner of the globe. Even the wind seems to bow before it, the treetops, cast in orange firelight, barely shivering in its dutiful howls as if recognising that the gale, like the grey hues of clouds, must come to an end.

The night is a time for silence. As the world shifts into twilight, there is no need for the distraction of nature, not when the sun is struggling to stay above the horizon, casting its orange light so high into the heavens. For now, there are no reds nor yellows, only the broken promise of pinks fluttering across the skyline, almost invisible to the naked eye. There's a warmth to the touch of colour brushing against the haze, the masterstrokes of an ageing painter, his works unfinished. Perhaps if they were brave enough, rather than dusty pinks and blues, we would see the same greens portrayed in an evergreen's leaves, the royal purple of a queen's finest gown. But there is something to be said for simplicity, for blue. The sky is no longer a blank contrast for the richness of the earth, standing as its own art, a watercolour shaded by the thin breeze. Soon, the night will awaken, the call of a far-off owl disturbing the peaceful slumber of men, the trees blackened by the midnight atmosphere. Blue will die like the grey of day, a final fantasy for the dwindling light. Perhaps we should worship these last moments, delight in the company of day, forget what notions the night will bring. Maybe the blue is our salvation, a salute to our warring nightmares, a triumph for all that is good. We cannot know what the dark will bring, but for now, in the mellow harmony of a fading sunset, there is blue.

Nan

There is something about a memory that is more beautiful than an independent thought, a shiver tingling down the intangible spine of history like water droplets shattering against a windowpane. Amongst the sunset there are hues of red and blue and yellow, the colours of the plastic roses sitting in her plant pot, her pale irises as the light faded from her eyes, the cracked paint that once tarnished the walls of her old home. It's gone now, a new coat painted on, set to dry like the broken pavements that once held her feet, the concrete giving way to green. I remember what she was before the life drained from her soul, a grandmother, a doting wife, so innocent in the infinite chaos battling just outside her door. Her hair wasn't always white, the colour of snowflakes melting upon rooftops, like snowmen in orderly lines, their scarves knitted by her ancient hands. She used to tell me stories of rabbits in blue cardigans, cats with striped hats exploring the last moments of a long-forgotten nation, living through the childish tales of freedom and lack of sacrifice. Always an undying martyr for her children, for her deceased husband, even as his bones lay sleeping in his grave. She loved him more than life itself; as a child, I could see the absence in her eyes, a heartbreak that couldn't be stitched together with knitting needles. We loved her so much, and maybe it wasn't enough, but there was pride in her eyes when she beheld our presence. This was what she made, what she left to the cruelties of this epic world. Even as her stars were smothered by clouds, burning in the melancholy twilight of her last stand, even when her few hopes became something akin to sorrow, she kept the last of her humanity next to her heart. Warring against the worst of a child's fantasies, armed with nothing more than a cup of sugary tea, we will remember. In our memories, she'll never truly be gone.

Age

It's easy to forget the truth when it's concealed behind tests and daydreams, a life wiped out, erased from the mind by devolution or war, subjunctives battling in the mind's eye. They say that to remember is to salvage a generation, wisdom lost through a receding hairline, squinting at the blurred pages of a book well-read. They don't think it is healthy to deal with grief without mourning, but I do mourn in the space between the lines, in the moments where I look up at my cracked ceiling and wonder why there are so many uncertainties in this universe, so many mistakes. I should have called her, should have said my final goodbye. Who knew that the last words I would ever say to her would be hidden behind a grim smile, that at the time, she was an inconvenience, a chore? I used to think her weak, hobbling around like an old crone, showing her age in her cracked teeth and dodgy hip. She wasn't perfect, and perhaps I already knew enough to look upon a false god's mighty creation and see its faults, but that doesn't mean I didn't resent her trespasses. Her image wasn't the stereotype of a kindly grandmother, baking cookies, letting me lick the spoon. I think I knew she was dying from the moment I saw her; as she abandoned her hair dye, her fussing, her movement, there was little I could give other than bland smiles, doing my best to ignore her condescending looks. I used to spend my time doing the sudoku in her morning paper, a brother or two next to me, chewing on a pen lid as I stared at a whirl of numbers, ignoring her completely. What did she think of me then? What would she think of me now, lost in the last sentences of a rambling story, trying my best not to think about the realities of the soul? I wish I could believe in God. I wish I could believe she was still here, reincarnated as the evergreen roses in her garden, a butterfly braving the cold air. I wish I could believe that she has found her way to heaven, reunited with her lost love, looking down on me with a wistful smile, remembering the wide-eyed child who would dance around the curiosity that stemmed from the pale roots of her hair, the fact that she walked a little oddly. But even in death's icy grip, perhaps I can believe that there's still warmth in her bones.

Dusk

There's a silence to the dawn, a contrast to the echoing of drums pounding in my head as I wake to the receding moonlight. Perhaps I hear the angels singing a resolute sound of victory, their hymns foreign in my dulled brain, like the words of some broken sonnet absent in my dreams. Maybe I should remember more about these moments, where blissful ignorance was nothing more than a fantasy, a shadow of a greasy nightmare, a soft voice playing over a telephone, shaking with all the feeling one finds absent in hatred. It's not resentment I feel, but beneath the darkness pooling through my spiteful giggles, I can see the mirror reflecting my heartache, a tightrope so thin that I fear I must fall into an abyss of suffering, plunging deep into the maddening reality of my soul. I don't know what I truly feel anymore, only what I'm meant to believe, my tattered gods running ragged across the dirt. Maybe the pain reflected in my eyes is visible, but beneath the moonlight, I can pretend that the whispers of the wind are her words, my coat her comforting touch, the fantasy only revealed by the amber glow of florescent stars, their man-made beauty a reminder of all I have lost. Even the clocktower seems silent, its ready chimes muted under my icy stare, magic dancing at my fingertips with the rage of a thousand lost souls. Perhaps the damned will hear me, calling out below the frozen lake, their hellish screams glistening like ripples on the surface. She won't be with them, the voice of a siren filled with empty temptation, calling out from the other side of the void, awaiting the weary in the hope of eternal sleep. But even as her ugly features repulse the worst of man, there is something in her passionate intensity that makes cowards of us all.

Faith

He watched the fire burn, glad for the amber light in the shadowy darkness, glittering embers sparkling as they reached for the blackened sky before smothering themselves in a thick cloak of ashen dust. In the bright gleam of the flames, he could see almost nothing, just the outlines of long-forgotten ruins, the last testament of a society lost in suffering. Staring at the heavens, he wondered if God could hear him now, if his dedicated worship had really been for nothing. The stars seemed to blink at him, mystical pinpricks of otherworldly desire, Aphrodite's last stand in a world waiting for something less than fear. This couldn't be it, the end of days fading from explosive atrocities, disappearing from tyrannical intensity. He'd waited for so long for his last judgement, but he could never have expected this. His fate seemed so cruel, to be alone with dead skeletons, only able to watch as darkness took hold of every sentient being, God but a whisper of the past. Where was he now? Humanity wasn't destroyed by corrupt governments, by mournful war nor starved famine. Death came in the arms of pestilence, a lover's touch, the end to the plague of insanity infesting the nations. Long ago, when he believed in something other than the warm embrace of deceased repose, he could ignore the faults of desolating reality, could focus on the word of the heavens. Now, he was sure that God had never spoken. Left with nothing but his solitary thoughts, he could no longer believe in his blessed faith. He could see that his omnipotent entity was little more than fiction, a human invention as extinct as he couldn't even pray to be. Nature had shown her true colours, playing on mankind's own arrogant stupidity, avenging her anguish. Humanity was victorious where it couldn't afford to win; in months she had managed what it could only dream. Soon, all of humankind would be wiped out, lost to the universe. His race had been conquerors once, wishing for peace through bloody war, holy in their advances, excusing their failures with their prayers. They fought for their damaged gods, cried for their dead but continued to slaughter, their missions worthless, their world filled with only violence and despair. It all seemed inconsequential: soon, they would be replaced only with rumours, murmurs of lost brilliance, survivors of crimson sacrifice. They sat, trapped in their caves, awaiting misery.

He thought of his past, the light hues of sunset before this never-ending darkness. He was meant to go on a pilgrimage once, a journey to honour his God. How worthless it seemed upon reflection, the adventure little more than a vague false memory. As his gaze fell back to the fire, he couldn't subdue the anger running through him. This wasn't the apocalypse he was promised. There would be no ascension, no hope, no love. Heaven was nothing but a lamented story, a dream he could never aspire to achieve. He could feel the world fading, no hate, no joy, no humanity. But still, he survived through the echoes of time, seeing molten angels where there was only dying ashes, fumes of putrid sorrow. If he would only listen, he would hear the long screams of the anguished, the sound of pain brought by the low rumble of broken machinery, gunshots billowing into the night. He'd been hunted for so long that it was easy to forget who he had once been, a priest, a murmur of kindness through the abandoned fog. He had watched the plague descend upon his people, watched how madness erupted between them, watched as the world plunged into chaos. What use was God when so many were dying? He hadn't thought, at least at first, that the disease had been anything important, a landmark in the history books that would never be written.

Perhaps, one day, when the last traces of humanity has been burned from the earth, there will be those that wonder what happened to their lost ancestors, but he knew now that there wasn't a person left worth saving. Anyone who had survived this long, who had defied all suffering, lingering in the hope that, somehow, order would be restored, had killed and murdered and maimed. Anyone who was still alive had only lived through anger and torment and fear. He had preached for peace once; how easily he had managed to forget that, to revert to his animalistic nature.

His clothes were stained crimson, drowned in a sea of desolate loss. There was blood under his fingernails, but he had long since stopped trying to pick it out, knowing that, sooner or later, he would just have to repeat the process. He had torn the throats of demons with his bare hands, cut them away from the shattered bodies they possessed. In the time before, he'd never believed in the existence of devils, but now he saw that they were just as man-made as the rest of creation. For a long time, he'd wondered whether he was held captive in his own mind, forced to do the things he'd done by evil hands, but not even Lucifer could have caused him to create such passionate intensity. He avoided mirrors, scared of his own reflection, sure that his very eyes would have turned black with cold malice, that hell was the only place for him now. But what else had Earth become? It was certainly no heaven, no pearly gates, no choirs singing. Perhaps he'd died with the first wave of pestilence, damned to this world for eternal punishment.

But in his heart, he knew it wasn't true. There was no excuse for the monster he had become, only proof for his eagerness to survive. At first, he'd acted only out of self-preservation, telling himself that things would, one day, be better, that he'd find his utopia, his Garden of Eden, that the world could get no worse. He watched as governments buckled, collapsing in an ocean of corruption, defeated by their ignorance, waiting for some kind of fictional hero. He had realised far too late that nobody was coming to save him. He was alone. Hymns of biblical misery became reality in front of his own eyes; the end of days was an ironic fantasy, a test of belief so terrible that the whole world stopped praying. The atheists were right, but there was no time for self-righteous gloating, their supercilious wisdom lost in the battle of the ages, the choking of the very foundations of the modern world. He had dreamed of salvation, then, relying on Pandora's final evil to vanquish the ghosts of hatred, uniting borders against the common enemy. But soon, even hope had left him, fluttering up into the heavens, receding from his blackening heart. Colour seemed to vanish, disappearing into gloomy greys, even the skies losing any tenuous grasp on oranges and yellows and blues. There was red, of course. Red running through the streets, drying on the pavements, soaking every inch of decay. Red polluting the seas, turning them crimson, red splattered across forests, massacres of the faithful left to rot between dying trees. He was waiting for the sky to change colour, to signify something close to biblical reasoning, but miracles have never been much use for cowards. That was what he was, what they all were. Cowards for not dying with the rest of them. Cowards for killing anybody who got in their way. Cowards for choosing to live in a world uninhabitable to anyone but the vilest of parasites.

In the distance, he could hear a child screaming. He hadn't seen a child in so very long, their numbers dwindling amongst men. Still, he didn't turn around, refusing to move an inch from his campfire, not even when the shriek was cut off abruptly, the crackling of his flames the only thing sparing him from complete silence. There were still humans, but humanity died a long time ago. They were worse than cannibals, prying on the weak for nothing more than another day in this inferno of torture. He would have to move soon: his supplies were dwindling, but he had found solace in the crumbling remains of an old home. There were faded photographs, a mother, a father, and two young girls, all of them smiling, all of them probably dead. He envied them: what use was living in wretchedness when he could be met by sweet oblivion? But he couldn't do it, chained by some long-lost hope, the belief in a beacon, a wandering sign of something other than life and death. There had once been more to living than outrunning groups of the walking dead, than sacrificing the unwary for necessary supplies, but those times seemed like nothing more than a distant memory. He had fallen in love, once, but he could barely remember her name. It wasn't important anymore. He was a dead man living, a zombie walking unsteadily on an injured foot, waiting to be claimed by a feeling more painful than bliss. He didn't notice his fire die, the glowing flames retiring to a place he wasn't brave enough to go, leaving him with only the sound of drastic silence.

Summer

Summer is the heat, the kind that sticks to your skin, beating down upon the sodden earth, each breath filled with the stench of humid air, damp with the sweat-soaked rags clinging like sellotape to each crevice, each dastardly wrinkle. The sky is blue, hard to see through the shine of the sun, yellow, almost unrecognisable without squinting through white or grey clouds, prominent against the horizon. There is something enveloping in the oppressive warmth flooding the air, an uncomfortable embrace of a piggish uncle, a blanket slightly too thick next to a raging fire. No proper work can occur on such days, the world too hot to function, the markets coming to a stop. Heat entraps the strongest of souls, a summer read and cool lemonade taking precedent over capitalistic nightmares, the sound of a neighbour's radio fuzzing vaguely in the background. A lazy day. Bright red burns cover the skin, blotches of colour in the places sun cream can't quite reach, a dalmatian drawn in pink hues. But whilst the end of summer cannot be foreseen, cracks appearing in the semi-perfect skyline. Rain will come, lightning shooting across the blue, white snow in the thickest of winters. Soon, the sun will disappear, the heat freeze; moth-eaten jumpers will be torn from the back of the wardrobe. Still, at this moment, the dying embers of summer thrive.

Bound By Love

He had loved her until soft tears poked at his eyes, a monster of his own creation, a beauty that would leave Aphrodite in the cold. Frankenstein had failed his monster, had abandoned it in a delirium that had lasted a lifetime. He would never make such a mistake. She was a perfect nightmare, a shadow on the lips of humanity. But he loved her still, his feeble beast. There was something magical within her, a spark on the fingertips, an ache that didn't quite relinquish its grip. In her eyes he would drown, icy blue like the colour of a frigid sky, melting slowly into a pool of green ivy. Love he found in power, in the charming smile, a ghost of a memory. She promised him the sweet embrace of death, a chilly cascade of love and danger, a reminder that old age would never claim him. Victory concealed itself behind fresh notions of a life he could never live, white-picket fences, driving to football games. It wasn't him, wasn't them. They loved in fire, burning for eternity in wicked graces, wishing for something more than to stay soundly alive. Without love, he was nothing, an ordinary man stuck in a world driven to ashes. There was no hope without the flames, the hot breath on his skin. Immortality stuck to them like it was branded with glue, another sunset returning in the same old hues. And yet, with her beside him, it was beautiful.

Rain

It's raining again, droplets spraying against the windowpane, flooding the life outside with a tinge of wetness, looking out upon a parallel world. Battering tears echo across the room, rattling against thunderstorms and chaotic lighting, sleep a far-away dream. The clouds, often a soft white, now transform to deep grey, visible behind the flashes of light striking down in diagonal stripes, a testament to the wrath of invisible gods. Beautiful. Perhaps humanity has failed them again, their anger terrible against the sky, or maybe the sticky heat of the past has wreaked havoc with autumn's rise. Evergreen trees fold under the weight of water, their leaves splintering, falling before their time, drifting away in the sighing breeze.

The rain does not make a sound until it hits the pavement. It plummets through the chilly air from a midnight sky, the stars smothered by grey smoke. Behind the inky black, illuminated by fluorescent streetlights, one could believe that the ethereal moon shines, reflecting the sun's warm gaze, turning it cold. Silence is broken by voices, fading personalities laughing into the depths of the night. In a moment, the world will sleep, subdued by the lull of the time, protected by red brick, charming toy houses standing proudly in a row. Secrets swill through the emptiness, streets cackling, cracking pavements lining the way for all the evils of human's foul temperament. The rain is forgotten, lost in the chaotic violence of the night.

The End

One day, the world will burn in an infinite blaze; society will collapse into a thousand pieces, like a puzzle ready to be undone. Splintering into man-made chaos, golden light will rain down upon the Earth, not in salvation, but like molten magma burning through the heart of human troubles, a testament to nature's last stand. Even before the solar flare, before the final silence, society will crumble, a fossil for the millennia of men. Fragments of time frozen in heat, extinction blazing bright, an echo of the fallen stars. One day, even as death perishes from the surface of a deceased world, as silence reigns supreme over a kingdom of dirt, as gods die and religion fails, still the universe will go on.

Time

Love is a punishment, a reminder of what can only be foreseen, of the marching tune of death's final victory. It's odd to think that one day, wrinkles will cover my skin like camouflage, hiding my soul beneath a grimace of aching joints, shocks of white hair protruding from a scalp used to gold. Perhaps my muscles will fail me, another old woman with a walking stick, a doting grandmother or aged adventurer, alone or beside a smiling partner, turning translucent as time refuses to slow. Maybe I am not meant for old age, a broken car and flashing lights, the world tumbling into inky black. We shall never know what day shall be our last, except, of course, for those practising man-made death, a mockery of sacred rites. Then again, I can see the appeal, mastering the second of two certainties in life. In pain there are consequences. In death there are none.
There was death in the arms of the sunlight as it danced into the dark, seeping gold hues stained with time. It's complicated, the ageing of the day, an old cup of tea turned lukewarm, an artist slowed by the seizing of hands, a clock ticking down the hours before the moon will rise. A

whirring, the sound of electronic machinery, unnatural in the centuries passed yet a marker of the now, of the aching advancements of a community disjointed in all but love. Power curses the worst, bleeding through into the youthful, an undercurrent to humanity's weakness. Whilst the world ends, there is sadness. Afterwards, there will be nothing but victory.

Icarus

Icarus laughed as he plummeted downwards, an expression of free-falling triumph, plunging towards the seas below. Burning wax melted across his skin, running over his blistered body, but there were no screams as he battled against the pain felt by only the dying. And yet it was nothing compared to where the sun reflected against the waters, turning them the same luminous gold that filled the sunset sky, tinged with the final colours of a king's touch. It couldn't compare to the countless mountains taunting the horizon, ancient castles smothered by green. He was going to die. He would perish in the ocean below, but he felt no fear, no anger towards his impending demise. If he cried out, he would ruin the beauty of his freedom, his final moments antagonised by a feeling he couldn't dare to comprehend. Helpless, mesmerised by the flickering dusk, he breathed in the cool air, determined for his last moments to be filled with splendour.

After the End

It is strange to believe that one day, the Earth will cease to exist, that the sun and the moon and the stars will be obliterated by the oncoming dawn. In the silence that will follow, there will be no blue skies, no rainy days. Death will be extinct, a strange silence lacing the air. Some believe it to be righteous, that sheep and goats are more than silly farm animals, that there is redemption at the end of all things. Perhaps they are right, their fantasies of primal goodness so much more infinitely promising than the constant black. After the end, maybe there will be something of which the gods could only dream, building blocks for another game, another constant torture of mortality. The legacy of man collapsed into less than dust, molten sparks dismissing the follies of creation. If God once knew the vivid truths of man, they have long since abandoned any sincerity as to their omnibenevolence. The world will end and so will everything in it, and yet there is still hope fluttering through the conscience of humankind.

Cycle

Love is a fickle thing, a twisting memory caught in the fantasies of childhood, an omen to the truth of human desires. One could believe it to be nothing more than a fairy-tale, a false hope to strive for, a meaning for a worthless life. Would we love if we did not know what it was? Would we feel our hearts flutter, butterflies soaring through our nerves? Do animals find love? I suspect not; love is a human invention, just as man-made as the written word.

But what are we without our own identified purpose? We work and we laugh, and we sleep, a cycle repeating for want of companionship, for a desire for change. If we do not love, we do not live in true harmony. We are not truly free.

There are a thousand things that control us, and yet, even as it chokes us, love runs free, weaving through a world of ads and rubbish, burning bright like Pandora's last evil. Perhaps through the miserable realisation of what we have become, it will be our salvation.

It

It's odd to be a woman in a world made for men, wisdom ignored due to a lilting tone. I think that there is an anger in all of us, bubbling up into a putrid façade of sardonic smiles, lined eyes bulging with contempt. Some hide it well, refusing to scream about the unfairities and insincerities, the promise of feminism floating behind an image of man-made inequality. Effortless. It is an effortless gesture to listen, to properly appreciate the opinions of half the human race. The world would be a better place if it just heard the billions of voices shouting out against the terror and gruesome tirade of a million years of pain. A man stared at my arse in the gym today. A man shouted after me on the street. A man made me feel like I am an object, a thing to fuck and clean and live in silence like my personality was a hindrance to their fantasies. Voiceless. Alone in a community lost to the hopeless arguments of timeless sorrow. This could be nothing more than a blip in tradition, a moment where the accomplishments of women are brought to the forefront, where movements have the capability for change. Our world is known for its dystopia, a climate crisis on the horizon, fools gaining traction through their absurdity. Wicked in the warming winds, it seems peculiar that no matter the life, each will die the same death in the end.

Power

Perhaps it is the disbelief that irks me, the sound of a child wailing for what it should always have, an increasing hatred for the powers one cannot control. They swear on their Bible, crying out for pathetic notions of their God, omnibenevolent, and yet, omnijudgemental. I have never truly believed in the righteous notions of the lost, unable to understand what seems like cultish coping mechanisms. There is nothing wrong with harmless teachings of love and faith, but the twisted words of vile justice mean nothing. To be a woman who loves another woman can be terrifying. To be a woman pregnant and alone with no choice but to bring a child into an unsufferable world is perverse. As The Handmaid's Tale draws ever closer, one must wonder how long it will be until women are silenced. Free speech means nothing when it is used to contradict and manipulate, to sign away the rights of another whilst their screams and hopes and dreams die, strangled by their misplaced freedom. Even as the world watches, waiting for the encore of backlash, a part of me dies inside, knowing that those voices weren't enough. Like the fantasies of the foul, the haunting ghost of the past, this sickening drivel smothers the last essence of hope for a world gone rogue.

Every Teenage Superhero

"Is that who you think I am?" She hissed, thunder rumbling somewhere in the darkness. "A coward? A witch? A peasant? I am nothing more than the hope that runs through your veins, the scattered wishes of a thousand nations. I am what the gods have always feared, a freedom to see and do and want for myself, a need to be something more than they want me to be. I can write my own sentences, form my own stories, think independently of the fallen angels. In my mind, I see the molten embers of creation, can fix the pleasant memories of our past. I'm meant to be dead, to have exploded into cinders before we ever met. I am a mistake. A test run that nobody ever thought to let die. Do you remember the stories we were told as children? Heroes slaughtered by ragged gods for entertainment, humanity a set of puppets dangling on threadbare strings. Maybe all that I can see and hear, and need was put here by some kindly deity, but as the world twists around me, all I can see is chaos and destruction and hate and I can't stand it anymore. Why save me? I never should have been born. I am no heroine, ready to battle for something more than peaceful massacres. I have no prophecy, no history of rebellion. I am not their leader, nor am I yours. I am just a girl out of place in her own time, a shadow in a moonlit night, shrouded in fickle mist. They need a soldier, a warrior to bring them, hope, to smash through the defences of a concrete city, to bring magic back from the brink of lesser evils. They shouldn't have chosen me. I never should have wanted to survive.

Effortless

There is a clarity in the conscious mind that brings a sort of self to us, an emotion so intense that it feels almost tangible behind our eyes. There's something in the fuzzy notion of breath, an icon so brilliant that it is often lost behind the spew of bias contorting our everyday vision. It's lost, here, now, to the acidity at the back of my tongue, a buzzing that one can't quite name, fear, perhaps. Or a longing for an unassociated thrill. In illegality is a certain beauty, a danger often rare to the forms of usual life. We see ourselves are we are defined by others, our lives contorting into beautifully controlled chaos, an ocean of nonsensical daydreams spilling out into the pit of our despair. But here, away from the wants of others, with stress melted away upon a hopeless daydream, reality does not seem so important anymore. In this world are a thousand things that could kill us, a million that could endanger our lives and a billion incredible notions of discovery of which we are yet to even scratch the surface. Why would you wait for a diamond in a legacy of tarnished emeralds? Why seek perfection in a moment of intrinsic harmony? We are all different people, different souls, come from different worlds, and yet we all share the same characteristics, troubles, fantasies. In a world made for so many, carved by so few, why would one choose to see consciousness only as of the way it is first perceived? One day, I shall die, and my body shall become an eternal flame, but it doesn't seem quite as important as the realisation that hope is nothing more than a sacrilege, a result of a thousand years of stagnated enterprise. If we hope, we fail to consider what is achievable, what we as a society can do to help cope with the jeopardy in which we are putting our future generations. I may hope for a better future, but that doesn't mean I can't strive to create it. I may live in a world of man-made starvation and melting icecaps, but that doesn't mean I have to drown in the increasing oceans when I can swim. I have read a thousand stories, and none of them has been from my point of view. Perhaps one day I should write something of my own, a treasure map aged in the faded print of old thoughts, a discovery for a time in which no deity can answer my timeless prayers. With cracked nail polish and a view of words that seem to distort with every blink, with every shadow of a reflection staring back at me, I write in the silence of a university campus known for its nightlife, the sound of each closing door slamming upon some jarred feeling in my conscience. I still see patterns in my carpet, although they're wearing thin, foreign laughter ricocheting off every seldom memory, a cascade of nonconformity falling so very far from grace. Effortless, a word stolen from me from some unknown author. Who would have thought that I am the same person now as that girl, a thousand levels shy of immaturity, a need to be seen as anything but a world of boring? Ironic, I suppose. I never should have worried. I think there's a level of deep thought that we find in our teenage years, a desire to be something other than the national trends brought upon us by the dying. We see it mocked on a global scale throughout the generations, and yet, who are we to judge? I would have become a different person in another time, I think, but then, I believe that some fundamental part of me would always be the same, something in the pitch of my laugh or the tone of my voice. In a trillion realities, a concept far too big for any of us to truly comprehend, there would always be some identifiable mark, a trace of a personality made from endless opportunities. I would be interested to know what it was, or whether across every set of stars, there's a different iconic set of features branded with my name. I've never been one to contemplate the finer gravities of life, out loud at least, but in a realm where magic is found only in the fingertips of writers, sometimes, one has to create a little of their own illusion. Certainty seems to be found often in science. There is a right answer to even the most intrinsic of questions, even if we are yet to find it, but in philosophy, theology, ethics? These schools of thought are often side-lined by the brash nature of a desire for resolute foundations in a world where reality is fundamentally obtuse; they are the finer points of mankind. If a society has grown to the point that they can have fat twats talking out of their arses about theories they know nothing about, civilisations that they are unable to help due to their unsettling lack of empathy, it is time for that culture to change. We are all flawed on an individual level; I am reminded of this by the smell of burnt toast flickering in the air, however, as the human race, we are completely detestable. We live in a rotting world talking about the harmful effects of toxins, of the issues of drugs on the poor, with no real answer of how we are to change it. Even our politics is corrupt, dividing us along a great valley in which lies a torrid inferno that no one dares cross, lest they are burned by the scathing opinions of their peers. I know for a fact that people are dying all over the world from a virus infecting the black hearts of the seven sins, know of the hoarding of resources as if stacks of dead bodies will simply dispose of themselves. It's like playing multi-story chess, where each level is each concern forced upon you by your semblance of reality, and you are forced to balance it without even the top-most pieces falling into an oblivion we are yet to comprehend. It is one of the most entitled feelings in the world to know that there are atrocities that need to be stopped and be angry at a deity that you don't believe in because all these horrible things are forced upon you, building up, like an unsteady breath, controlling you through environmental circumstances even though you never asked for any of this. It is not my fault that everything is exactly how it is, not up to me to change it. If my single life is forgotten on this earth, then it makes no difference to the universe. If it is remembered across all of space and time, then it makes a difference to me.

Cold

It's snowing outside. I can feel it, the shiver scaling my bones, climbing my ribs as if there were rungs of some grotesque ladder, the cold seeping into my skin. The birds don't seem to mind it, chirping along to the merry breeze, watching the sun fade from the sky behind a cloud of grey. The lamplights have been switched on illuminating the street with their fluorescent glow, fresh white pavements soon to be turned to slush. I remember counting each amber shine on my paper round, awaiting the moment I could return home.

Home. A funny word. Home can't protect me from the cold. It shelters me from the cold, but my clothes still feel damp against my skin. The doorbell rings from down below. It's not for me, but then, it rarely is. At this time of evening, nothing arrives but the midnight sky. There's an electronic whirring fiddling with my silence, the birds still whispering in their trees. What is sanity but a socially constructed view, an unachievable brush with some deity's view of creation? If we were made in the image of God, then God himself is royally fucked up. We are all lost, walking in shadows, awaiting the next sunrise, the next out of daylight before we are left alone. The radio is playing again. I've never really liked it, the repetitive songs from a time where my existence wasn't much more than a thought. There doesn't seem to be much point to radio, not anymore, but the death of such a thing seems dire. The snow's stopped, but the shower has turned on, hot water cascading through the steamy air, a seldom tear falling deep into misery.

www.ingramcontent.com/pod-product-compliance
Lightning Source LLC
Chambersburg PA
CBHW051746130826
49812CB00033B/1027
* 9 7 8 9 3 5 7 4 4 5 2 3 8 *